EMINƎM

Survivor

Publisher and Creative Director: Nick Wells
Project Editors: Polly Prior and Catherine Taylor
Picture Research: Laura Bulbeck and Alexandra McClean
Art Director and Layout Design: Mike Spender
Digital Design and Production: Chris Herbert

Special thanks to: Stephen Feather and Karen Fitzpatrick

FLAME TREE PUBLISHING
Crabtree Hall, Crabtree Lane
Fulham, London SW6 6TY
United Kingdom

www.flametreepublishing.com

First published 2012

12 14 16 15 13
1 3 5 7 9 10 8 6 4 2

Flame Tree Publishing is part of The Foundry Creative Media Co. Ltd

A CIP record for this book is available from the British Library upon request.

ISBN 978-0-85775-277-2

Printed in China

EMINƎM

Survivor

MICHAEL AND DREW HEATLEY

FOREWORD: PRIYA ELAN, ASSISTANT EDITOR, NME.COM

**FLAME TREE
PUBLISHING**

CONTƎNTS

FOR3WORD

Eminem started off as the outsider: the kid on welfare who moved from home to home; the victim of bullying who survived a brain haemorrhage; the white rapper trying to make it as a legitimate hip-hop act when there had been no precedent. The odds were stacked wholly against him, and yet he made it through a sheer force of will and the power of his unique artistic vision.

The outsider became the insider as Eminem turned a lifetime's worth of pain and anger into great art. His monstrous side became the cheeky alter-ego 'Slim Shady', his lyrics reflected on the tumult of his life in a style that some called Shakespearean. In fact, he changed the face of pop music (and music video) in the process. Through his decade-plus career, he has gone from being the exception to the rule to tearing up the rulebook completely.

Eminem, Survivor tells his compelling, utterly unique tale; how he threaded all his issues into his boundary-pushing music; through his increasingly inventive music videos, his deeply autobiographical (and acclaimed) performance in *8 Mile*, along with his lyrics which poked a much-needed finger of fun at the world of celebrity. The book provides an enthralling overview of his career via bite-sized chunks of text and career-defining pictures. 'Will the real Slim Shady please stand up?' Eminem once asked rhetorically. Well, you'll find him here in the pages of this book.

Priya Elan, Assistant Editor
www.NME.com

IDƎNTITY
CRISIS KID

Eminem, **Marshall Mathers** and **Slim Shady** are all one and the same person – the first rap superstar of the twenty-first century who made his first impact in the final year of the twentieth. But the man who borrowed the name of a chocolate sweet as his rap tag is no soft centre. Sometimes the limelight has been too much for him, leading him to wish he could come off stage, turn off the spotlight and just be Marshall Mathers again.

'Marshall Mathers is a regular person, Eminem is a nice guy and Slim Shady is a complete d*©k. Who's the smartest? Eminem. Who's the loser? Marshall. Who's the winner? Slim Shady.'

EMINEM

'We were on welfare, and my mom never worked. There were times when friends had to buy me f#©*in' shoes! I was poor white trash, no glitter, no glamour, but I'm not ashamed of anything.'

EMINEM

He has battled many demons, from substance abuse to depression, yet has managed to keep a hold on sanity as well as stardom. Three identities have, at times, seemed to cook up three times as much trouble – but whatever you choose to call him, Eminem is a giant of rap music with millions of fans hanging on his every word.

LIFE ON THE RUN

Eminem was born Marshall Bruce Mathers III on 17 October 1972 and raised on the seamy side of Detroit by his teenage mother, Debbie. He never knew his father, who left when he was five or six months old. At the age of five the family moved to a bad part of Detroit, but Marshall was picked on at school, and so the family moved back to Kansas City, then back to Detroit again when he was 11 years old. His mother had another child, his half-brother Nathan, so when the family moved back to Michigan they stayed wherever they could, with his grandmother or whichever relative could put them up. His mother tried to do the best she could, but moving every two or three months meant Marshall would attend several different schools in one year.

INTO THE MUSIC

Life on welfare and constantly moving home to escape the bailiffs was stressful, so Marshall found his escape route in rap and hip-hop music. He had a guide in Uncle Ronnie, a family member who was like the big brother he never had. He knew

lots about music and became Marshall's mentor. The first rap record the teenager ever heard was 'Reckless' by Ice-T. 'I just started getting into it, breakdancing and s#!t like that. It just elevated from there as rap started going on.' At 15 or 16 years old he started wanting to rap and began writing lyrics: 'I hated school. I just wanted to rap. I'd go to friends' houses and rap, or I'd stay in my room all day, standing by the mirror and lip-synching songs, trying on different clothes, trying to look cool.'

TOO COOL FOR SCHOOL

School was a constant trial for the young Marshall Mathers, and at the age of 15 one of numerous beatings almost proved fatal: a brain haemorrhage put him in a coma for nine days. Unsurprisingly, he dropped out of the education system for good after failing his ninth grade three times. The relationship with his mother soured, his beloved Uncle Ronnie committed suicide and Marshall got his girlfriend Kim pregnant: what else could go wrong? Happily, the birth of his daughter Hailie Jade on Christmas Day 1995 would ultimately be the best moment of his life.

His response to adversity was to move into music as an MC, though he experienced considerable resistance from those on the (predominantly black) scene. Even so, he persevered, recording a now hard-to-find first album, *Infinite* (1996), for a local label. He didn't know it then, but he was on the first step of the ladder to stardom.

The first time I grabbed the mic at the Shelter, a Detroit MC club , I got dissed. I only said, like, three words, and I was already gettin' booed. I started getting scared, like, is this gonna happen? Am I gonna make it or not?' EMINEM

TALKING INTO TROUBLE

Eminem had begun rapping with a high-school friend at age 14, the pair adopting the rap names 'Manix' and 'M&M', the latter of which soon morphed into Eminem. Under this name, Marshall started battle rapping, a struggle that would later be dramatized in the movie *8 Mile* (2002).

His outspoken style, voiced through his other identity of Slim Shady, quickly won him many enemies. His dislike of gay men attracted much critical flak, while references to his mother in the hit single 'My Name Is' led to a multi-million-dollar lawsuit. Meanwhile, an ongoing argument with wife Kim (which also led to a summer 2000 lawsuit) also found its way into song '97 Bonnie And Clyde'. Every way he turned there was trouble …

STRENGTH IN NUMBERS

Marshall's fast-growing rapping skills soon began to earn him a reputation, and he was invited to join several groups. The first of these was the New Jacks and, after they disbanded, he joined Soul Intent – they released a single ('F#*©!n' Backstabber') on the Mashin' Duck record label in 1995. This single also featured Proof and the two broke away to form their own posse: D-12, a six-member crew that functioned more as a Wu-Tang-style collective than a regularly performing group.

The outfit featured six MCs, aged between 23 and 25, each with two identities like Eminem and Slim Shady. These were

'Slim Shady is just the evil thoughts that come into my head. Things I shouldn't be thinking about. A lot of my songs are funny. I got a warped sense of humour I guess.' EMINEM

Bizarre, Proof, Kon Artis, Kuniva and Bugz. The unfortunate Bugz was shot dead in 1998 and replaced by Swifty McVay. D-12 stood for their 'Dirty Dozen' identities – and when Eminem started his own label, Shady Records, in partnership with Interscope, they were his first signing.

INFINITE

The first recording Eminem made, *Infinite*, was a cassette tape, released only in Detroit, in 1996, to capitalize on the response he was getting live. Only 1,000 tapes were pressed up and most sold, though the original investors didn't make their money back.

'**Infinite** was me trying to **figure out** how I wanted my **rap style** to be, how I wanted to **sound** on the **mic** and **present myself.** It was a **growing stage.**' EMINEM

It has since been made available on the internet in bootleg form. Eminem himself has disowned it and doesn't count it as his first album, claiming that, as it was cut just before his daughter was born, he had other things going on and was therefore less than committed to it. He said, 'I felt like *Infinite* was like a demo that just got pressed up.'

The hip-hop style of *Infinite* copies the rhyming of Nas or AZ. Producer Mark Bass felt the failure of *Infinite* was due to the fact that people weren't ready to see a white hip-hop artist.

RAPPING AND RHYMING

An appearance at the 1997 Rap Olympics in Los Angeles saw Eminem controversially cheated of victory, but the experience nevertheless helped him make a crucial connection with former N.W.A man Dr. Dre. The entrants' names were supposed to go into a hat, and two rappers get picked out to battle each other with whatever came into their heads. Then the crowd would decide who the winner was, a panel of judges stepping in if the outcome was unclear. When someone came up to Eminem afterwards and asked him for a demo tape, he gave it to him, little knowing it would be played for record producer Jimmy Iovine. Jimmy played it to Dr. Dre and the resulting album, *The Slim Shady LP* (1999), cut in just two weeks of studio time, would change not only Marshall Mathers' life but the face of rap music.

'In my entire career in the music industry, I have never found anything from a demo tape of a CD. When Jimmy (Iovine) played this, I said, "Find him. Now!"' DR. DRE

A LOVƎ-HATE RELATIONSHIP

Marshall's on-and-off relationship with Kimberley Scott began in 1989 when they met in high school. She fell pregnant with their daughter, Hailie Jade Mathers, who was born on Christmas Day 1995. The couple married in 1999 and divorced two years later, but remarried in January 2006. Their second divorce was finalized in December that same year, the couple agreeing to share custody of their daughter.

'One time we came home and Kim had thrown all his clothes on the lawn. So Em's like "I'm leaving her; I'm never going back." Next day, he's back with her. The love they got is so genuine, it's ridiculous. But there's always gonna be conflict.' DJ PROOF

Theirs was a rocky relationship, and it often spilled over into Eminem's songs like '97 Bonnie & Clyde'; his attempt to get back at Kimberley when she was trying to keep him from seeing his daughter. 'It's better to say it on a record than to go out and do it,' he reasoned of its threatening lyric. About the song 'Kim', he says, '[It's] like an outtake from one of our arguments in everyday life. That's really how we fight sometimes.'

CRY FOR HELP

Before he made money from music, Marshall had a string of dead-end jobs. 'I had a couple of cook jobs, short-order cook and s#!t; factory jobs, sweeping floors and cleaning toilets and s#!t. Just s#!^y f#©&in' bulls#!t jobs.'

The song 'Rock Bottom' tells the story of when Marshall had been fired from his chef's job at Gilbert's Lodge five days before Christmas. It was also daughter Hailie's birthday and he had just 40 dollars in his pocket to get her something. 'That was the worst time ever. I wrote "Rock Bottom" right after that.' It told the story of a suicide attempt that was more a cry for help. 'I was like, "I'm 23 years old, I'm not goin' to get a record deal, s#!t is not going to work out."' Happily, things were to take a turn for the better in a matter of weeks.

MARSHALL AND MOM

If Marshall's relationship with girlfriend/wife Kim was up and down, then the one with his mother, Debbie, has proved even

'I was in the studio one night and swallowed a bunch of pills. I had to get my stomach pumped. I threw up all over my man's basement studio. The funny thing is, less than a month later Dre called...' EMINEM

more of an emotional rollercoaster. As soon as he turned 15, he claims his mother told him to 'get a job and help me with these bills or your ass is out'. 'Then she would f#©^ing kick me out anyway, half the time right after she took most of my paycheck.' References to his mother in the hit single 'My Name Is' and *The Slim Shady LP* led to a multi-million-dollar lawsuit for defamation. She sued him for around $10 million and won only about $1,600 in damages in 2001. Theirs is clearly a love-hate relationship, as he said in one of his mellower moods: 'My mother and my little brother are really like the only family I got.' Maybe she was happy that the glamorous Kim Basinger was cast to play her in the autobiographical movie *8 Mile*.

PRIVATE PARENTHOOD

Since Marshall Mathers did not know his own father, it would be easy to guess that parenthood might not have come naturally to him. Yet, raising his half-brother Nathan, born when he was 11 years old, helped him cope with the birth of his own daughter. When Hailie was born, he found he was able to cope quite naturally. His initial fear was that he wouldn't be able to raise her and support her as a father should, and was tormented that for her first two Christmases she would find nothing of any value under the tree. However, when she turned three, she had more than enough presents to make up for it.

Eminem says he will never write a song about his love for his daughter, calling those 'private feelings' – but there is little doubt she is number one in his life. He admits he can't stop himself from spoiling her. 'My family is all I have ever fought for,' he says, 'and all I've ever tried to protect.'

'I did this so that I could be a family to Kim and Hailie and raise my daughter the right way and not cut on her like my father did to me. The only thing I'm scared of is being taken away from my little girl.'

EMINEM

SCHOOL OF RAP

Being from Detroit, Eminem found himself midway between the East Coast and West Coast schools of rap. The East Coast was predominantly known for its lyrics and the West Coast was equally famous for its gangsta attitude. He aimed to mix the two and 'get something crazy' – and that's exactly how it turned out once he had served his apprenticeship at the school of rap. At 15 or 16 years old, he admits he was 'wack'. He says, 'I didn't know how I wanted to sound, I didn't know anything.' Three or four years later, he knew exactly how he should sound on the mic. It was when learning how to battle, practising freestyle, that he became known in the Detroit underground scene. A couple of years later, Eminem would be a household name. Since he was a little kid, he had wanted to be an entertainer: it was the fulfilment of a dream.

LONDON TO MANCHESTER

Eminem made his first London performance at the Subterranea nightclub in March 1999. He came on stage thinking it was going to be a music-industry showcase full of men in suits, but was happy to find that 'True heads were in the crowd giving me love and it made me feel good.' The crowd were rapping along with him, creating an effect that was 'off the hook, man!'

Ironically, two years later he would be met by 100 demonstrators as he kicked off the first of three UK concerts. Protesters demanded he 'stop the bigotry, stop the hate' as 15,000 fans attended the show in Manchester, protesting at

'The show was dope! It's the first time I've been in London and I've been waiting for the moment to give some love back to all the people that have been showing me love in the UK. The s#!t was real!' EMINEM

his anti-gay lyrics. However, the audience, among which were Manchester United footballer David Beckham and his wife, Spice Girls singer Victoria, enjoyed what they heard.

NO ROLE MODEL

Eminem insists he is not a role model, and has never claimed to be. His music isn't for younger kids to hear and, since all his albums have an advisory sticker on them, you must be 18 to buy them. It doesn't mean younger kids won't be exposed to it, but he strongly believes he can't be held responsible for every kid out there who misbehaves.

'I don't think music can make you kill or rape someone any more than a movie is going to make you do something you know is wrong, but music can give you strength. It can make a 15-year-old kid, who is being picked on by everyone and made to feel worthless, throw his middle fingers up and say, "F#©k you, you don't know who I am."' In essence, music can help make them assert their individuality, which is exactly what it did for the young Marshall Mathers.

'People ask me, "What would you say to someone that wanted to grow up to be like you?" And I would say not to do it. Don't grow up to be me. But, at the same time, is it really a bad thing to grow up to be like me, to come from the gutter and become a rap star?'

EMINEM

'My album is so autobiographical that there shouldn't really be any more questions to answer. It's the story of a white kid who grew up in a black neighborhood who had a pretty s#!**y life ... not the worst life in the world, but still a fairly s#!**y life.' EMINEM

THE SLIM SHADY LP

If his personal life was a mess, Eminem could at least look to a blossoming career. *The Slim Shady LP* won a Grammy for best rap album of 1999, and reached No. 12 in Britain and No. 2 in his native US. As a result, Missy Elliott, the most respected female rapper around, invited Eminem to record with her – a much appreciated seal of approval.

Eminem's first album opened a lot of doors for him to push freedom of speech to the limit. It basically told the story of his life so far, so it was no surprise that things came easily. In his first day in the studio, Eminem recorded three songs (including the mega hit-to-be 'My Name Is') in six hours. Producer Dr. Dre was astonished at the rate of progress, but the newcomer was anxious to show what he could do.

'This is more of a feel album. You can feel these songs more than laugh at them. I say whatever I want to say, whatever is on my mind. If I get sued, if I get beat up, happens, nobody's gonna stop me saying what I wanna say.' EMINEM

TOP OF THE POPS

The Marshall Mathers LP (2000) shot to the very top of the transatlantic charts and contained three major hits in 'The Real Slim Shady', 'Stan' (both UK chart-toppers) and 'The Way I Am'. It sold 1.76 million copies in its first week, breaking the records set by Snoop Dogg's *Doggystyle* (1993) as the fastest-selling hip-hop album and Britney Spears' *...Baby One More Time* (1999) as the fastest-selling solo album in US chart history.

Dr. Dre, who did three tracks on the previous album, was far more involved in the making of this one. The trademark anger and sarcasm we now associated with Eminem was in full effect as he aimed to improve on his previous effort – and did so. 'If you don't make your album better than your last one,' he said, 'then you shouldn't even be in the game.'

ANGER MANAGEMENT

A Stateside tour in October 2000 with Limp Bizkit, dubbed the Anger Management Tour, pulled sell-out crowds and confirmed Eminem as star of the year. Targeted at both rap and rock fans, it also featured Papa Roach and proved so successful that a second tour happened in 2002, but without the now-headlining Limp Bizkit, and a third in the summer of 2005 with 50 Cent.

Tour one kicked off in New Jersey in mid-October and stormed through the US for the next two months, finally ending up in Jacksonville, Florida, just before Christmas. The only shadow on Eminem's success was cast by his arrest

on suspicion of carrying a concealed weapon – a problem preventing him from fulfilling planned British festival dates. The European leg of the Anger Management Tour finally took place in February 2001, and was filmed for later video release as *All Access Europe*.

THE DIRTY DOZEN

It can get a little lonely being a solo star, so when Eminem started his own label, Shady Records, in partnership with Interscope and with the help of his manager Paul Rosenberg, in late 1999, his first signing was rap group D-12 – of which he was of course a member. They immediately made their mark with the US chart-topping *Devil's Night* album (2001) and the singles 'S#!t On You', 'Purple Pills' and 'Fight Music'. All expletive-filled playground rhymes, it lacked Eminem's clever wordplay, but he clearly enjoyed the chance to goof off in the company of his homies. After their debut, D-12 took a three-year break from the studio, later regrouping to release second album *D-12 World* (2004), but two years later D-12 member (and Eminem's childhood friend) DJ Proof (DeShaun Holton) was shot and killed in a Detroit club.

INSPIRATION STRIKES

Ideas for songs come to Eminem when he is in bed waiting to sleep, or if he overhears people talking. The way people put words together is what inspires him. When he writes his songs, he writes the verses first and then sums them up with a chorus or 'hook'. He is a perfectionist and is only happy

'Whenever I go to England or Germany people always ask "Do you like the country so far?", but I don't get to see anything. I get to see the inside of rooms, talk to people, take pictures, then do a show.' EMINEM

when what he comes up with is something he can listen to 'a million times and not find a flaw'. When he writes a song, he usually uses the truth as the foundation and then mixes it with a little imagination.

He writes on a sheet of paper, scattered with ideas, words and metaphors, and when he has enough ideas, he pieces the song together. When he writes, he starts at the corner of the paper and writes at a slanting angle – he has no idea why.

'D-12 is just gritty. My s#!t is kind of sarcastic and political and Dirty Dozen s#!t is on some criminal type s#!t, you know what I'm sayin'? They're on some more gun-bustin' and shootin' and stabbin' s#!t, a little more so than I am, if you can believe that.' EMINEM

'I hate cleaning up lyrics for radio. I cringe every time I gotta do it. But I got a choice. I could refuse, meaning that it would never hit radio and I wouldn't have as big a voice in hip-hop as I wanna have.'

EMINEM

RECORDING PERFƎCTION

Eminem is always very focused when recording. When he has written a song he records his vocals in a day and takes the tape home to listen to it overnight. He then does more vocals the following day. He might have the skeleton of the song, the vocals and the beat down for a full two months before he puts the finishing touches to it, such as sound effects or dropping the beat out.

'When I record I slip into the zone. I don't like to talk a lot. I like to stick to myself and get my thoughts together, think how I'm gonna map out each song.' EMINEM

His guide to the studio was Dr. Dre, real name Andre Young, who found fame in the 1980s with influential gangsta-rappers N.W.A with Eazy-E, Ice Cube, MC Ren and DJ Yella. His solo debut album *The Chronic* (1992) won a Grammy, so he was an ideal role model for Eminem to follow. He is also a

perfectionist and is known to pressure the artists he produces to give flawless performances. Clearly the pair were singing from the same rap song sheet.

STAN THE FAN

These days Eminem interacts with his fans via social media, but back in the day his constant stream of fan mail provided him with the inspiration for a bestseller. The 2000 UK No. 1 single 'Stan' is about an obsessed fan who keeps writing to Eminem and tells him he takes everything he says literally.

The song was based on real letters the rapper had received, showing the way people perceived him. Eminem claimed he read almost every fan letter he received but didn't have time to write back. Sadly, the song ends with the disillusioned, unanswered fan ending it all. 'The plot is that I don't have time to write back to this guy so he thinks I'm dissing him and finally at the end of the song I write back not knowing he's killed himself.' Nowadays, Em's six million followers on Twitter can now access their hero more speedily.

MAKING PLANS FOR DIDO

One artist who has good reason to thank Eminem is Dido, alias of British trip-hop singer Florian Cloud de Bounevialle Armstrong. She was more or less unknown until Eminem introduced her to his audience in 2000 by sampling the first verse of her 'Thank You' in 'Stan'. She repaid the favour when she agreed to appear in the music video as Stan's long-

'I get a lot of **fan mail** … some of it's **normal** and some of it's **crazy.** I'm a **crazy guy,** not clinically **insane,** but **crazy,** so I attract a lot of **weirdos.** You can't control who **likes you.'** EMINEM

"'My Name Is...' blew up commercially, but we had no plans for that. We just thought it was a hot song and we put it out. Now, you've got underground kids talking s#!t about me like I'm a pop artist because I made one song that was catchy.' EMINEM

suffering girlfriend. There was a problem when Eminem revealed she would have to be tied up and gagged, but to her relief most countries' television channels did not show that version of the promo. Her debut album *No Angel* (1999), which contained the track, charted in Britain on the strength of import copies even though it had yet to be issued there. Eminem would return to the Dido catalogue in 2004, sampling the track 'Do You Have A Little Time' on the song 'Don't You Trust Me?' by Tupac on the album *Loyal To The Game* (2004), which he produced.

'MY NAME IS...'

The first single from Eminem's major label debut album, *The Slim Shady LP,* proved 'really simple to write'. He says, 'I thought of the hook right away, even before I wrote the song.' Musically 'My Name Is…' used a sample of a track called 'I Got The…' by British singer-songwriter Labi Siffre who insisted on lyrical approval before he approved the use of his music.

The song made No. 2 in Britain and No. 36 in the US, making music history by making Eminem the first rapper to reach the top spot on MTV's Total Request Live (TRL). Its popularity did not please Eminem, however, who later called it 'bubblegum rap'. The video, which did so much to make the song popular on MTV, showed a couple in a trailer (mobile home), similar to the one Marshall Mathers grew up in, watching clips on TV: these included Eminem impersonating president Bill Clinton.

FAME AND WƎALTH

Eminem admits he can't trust anyone he meets unless they knew him as Marshall Mathers. He says he is suspicious in case they are 'hanging out with me because I'm a celebrity or they think they can get something from me'. Manager Paul Rosenberg feels he has handled fame well. 'He has fun, but he's not out of control.' One thing that helped, Rosenberg believes, was that because Em didn't have experience with money he was scared to spend it. 'He doesn't know what the hell to do with it … His idea of splurging is spending $500 or $600 at Nike Town.'

'I went from not being able to afford nothing to limitless money, almost. I have more than I know what to do with. I can buy my daughter anything she wants, any time she wants it. And that's the best feeling in the world.' EMINEM

For laughs, Eminem has occasionally gone back to former workplace Gilbert's Lodge in a limo: 'Just for the spite of it, hop out, go to the bar, drop a couple of hundred dollars for a tip and throw it in their faces. They took me for a joke, but now the joke's on them.'

SWEET HOME DETROIT

Eminem has always remained loyal to his home city of Detroit, declaring, 'Los Angeles is a fun place to visit (to record) but I don't think I could ever leave Detroit, I got too much history there, too many roots.' It wasn't always like that; he found himself resented in his neighbourhood because of his fame and also because he was white. 'Then I caught some dude breaking into my house for, like, the fifth time, and I was like, "Yo, f#©k this! It's not worth it. I'm outta here."'

On that day, he vowed to get a house in the suburbs. He even stopped writing for five or six months and was about to give music – and Detroit – up. Instead, he stuck it out, sucked up the abuse and put all his frustration into his music.

LOVING LIVE WORK

Eminem has a work ethic like no other. 'I like to work for my money,' he says. 'I like to go out and entertain crowds because it makes me feel like I'm working.' It's never been enough for him to stand there and soak up the adulation – he has to give a show. 'I want to entertain people. I want

'If the crowd is making no noise, I'm going to address it. If they ain't making no noise, I'm going to stop my record – "Yo, you ain't feeling me?" or whatever. If they're throwing s#!t and acting rowdy, I address it.' EMINEM

to talk to people, keep eye contact with the people. And really just try to see what they're feeling.' The people buying his records are important and he's determined to keep in touch with them.

But things have changed a little over time. The days of chainsaws and gimp masks seemed well and truly over when, in 2011, his festival rider reportedly demanded a wooden pond in the backstage area filled with expensive koi carp. Other items supposedly on his rider included dumbbells, a microwave, seedless watermelon and yogurt.

'THE WAY I AM'

Eminem wrote 'The Way I Am' in response to his record label Interscope's demands for a bestselling first single from his album. He had finished recording but they didn't hear a sure-fire hit. He admits he was feeling the frustration and pressure of trying to top 'My Name Is', so right after meeting the label he wrote the song as a message 'to get off my f#©*in' back'.

In the end, it was the second single from *The Marshall Mathers LP*, following 'The Real Slim Shady', and it made No. 8 in Britain; curiously it did not even reach the Top 50 back home in the US. It was the first time Eminem had produced himself unassisted. The song's later remix by Danny Lohner featured Marilyn Manson, who has performed the song with Eminem live on stage – even though Em had poked fun at him on the video for 'My Name Is'.

'I had my whole album just about finished. I went up to Interscope and played it. But everybody was saying they didn't feel like I had a lead-off single – they were all second singles, like "Stan" and "Criminal".'

EMINEM

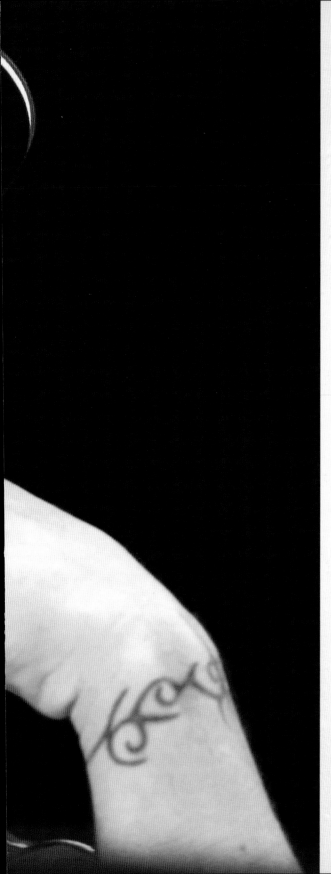

THE EMIN∃M SHOW

Eminem's third full-length album, *The Eminem Show*, effortlessly shot to the top of the charts in the summer of 2002. However, this was the year the mass adoption of the internet was approaching fever pitch, and while the net would provide the public with invaluable tools such as email, it would also enable people to leak material online, and spawned services such as peer-to-peer file-sharing networks, which fostered the illegal downloading of content. Eminem would experience this for the first time with *The Eminem Show*.

The album was leaked online ahead of its scheduled release date, despite being touted as one of the most closely guarded releases in the history of music. In an attempt to foil the illegal sharers, Eminem's label, Interscope Records, pushed the album's US release forward with the hastily assembled marketing tagline 'America Couldn't Wait'. However, there was no doubt Marshall Mathers was seething.

AMERICA COULDN'T WAIT!

In spite of its internet leak, *The Eminem Show* still stormed to No. 1 – a fact all the more remarkable since it had hit stores on a Sunday in late May, just one day before the Billboard chart figures were compiled. The album's success was proof of the appetite for Eminem's music, and showed that not even the more unsavoury aspects of the internet could keep him down. The album was eventually certified diamond in the US, shifting more than 10 million units there.

The Eminem Show followed in the footsteps of The Slim Shady LP and The Marshall Mathers LP by winning a Grammy Award, making Eminem the first artist to win Best Rap Album for three consecutive releases. It was also the bestseller of 2002, thanks to the hit singles 'Without Me', 'Cleanin' Out My Closet', 'Sing For The Moment' and 'Superman'. The last-named even managed to reach the Top Ten without a widely available video. The first two million copies of the album shipped in the US included a bonus DVD with an exclusive interview and live footage, while The Eminem Show was Em's first album to include lyrics to all the songs inside the CD booklet.

VIDEO KILLED THE RADIO STAR

Throughout his career, Eminem has been known just as much for his videos as for his music – sometimes funny, sometimes thought-provoking, but always entertaining. His music videos would become a mainstay on TV channels such as MTV, and later YouTube. The lead single from The Eminem Show, titled 'Without Me', would be no different.

Eminem drafted famed music video director Joseph Kahn to film the tongue-in-cheek video that sees him and Dr. Dre, as superheroes, trying to stop a child buying Eminem's music. The video also includes a scene where Eminem plays US dance musician Moby as part of an ongoing feud, and even includes terrorist Osama Bin Laden just over a year after the atrocities of 9/11. But Eminem was no stranger to controversial videos, and it appeared fans and critics alike loved it; the video has clocked up more than 50 million views on YouTube and won a Grammy in 2003.

'I picture this scrawny little dickhead going "I got Eminem's new CD! I'm going to put it on the internet." Anybody who tries to make excuses for that s#!t is a f#©*ing bitch.' EMINEM

SPLITTING THE NATION

As an international superstar, Eminem is aware that everything he does – no matter how small – will be scrutinized on a global scale. He knows that now. Perhaps he didn't know it in 2002 at the MTV Video Music Awards, when comments he made while accepting an award for Best Male Video for 'Without Me' split the nation. Fans and critics alike took to the internet to voice their opinion.

Continuing his feud with Moby, who was in the crowd, Marshall called him a 'little girl' and said 'I will hit a man in glasses'. The room filled with boos and millions at home frantically tapped their computer keys. One girl branded him a bully, another claimed he had 'ruined the night'. However, others called it 'classic Eminem' and 'the artist we fell in love with', proof that you can't please everybody all the time.

'We were **initially** going to make some sort of **slick-looking** video with **movie-like** production values. **Eminem** was going to just look **cool**, and in **no way** was he going to wear a **silly** costume or make a **fool** out of **himself. Oops.'**

JOSEPH KAHN

'**I honestly,** in all sincerity, thought that the whole **thing** was done in **some** semblance of **humor** until Eminem … threatened to **beat me up** … I'm stunned at the **anger** that he has **for me.'** MOBY

ANGER MANAGƎMENT ENCORE

The first Anger Management Tour of the States in the autumn of 2000 with Limp Bizkit and Papa Roach proved such a success that a second leg was launched in the summer of 2002. Fred Durst and company were otherwise engaged, but as Eminem explained to *Launch* magazine, he still planned to have fun. 'It's basically the same thing that it was the last Anger Management Tour without Limp Bizkit… Papa Roach are still cool, though.'

Kicking off in Buffalo in mid-July, the tour ended in Detroit in early September. In 2005 a DVD of the performance in Eminem's home town on the last night of the tour was released and features behind-the-scenes footage as well as special guests D-12 and Obie Trice. The 20 songs featured spanned his entire career, starting with *The Slim Shady LP* and through to the then-current *The Eminem Show*. The D-12 crew joined in on numbers such as 'Fight Music' and 'Purple Pills', while the audience often gets in on the action too. Highlights include 'Without Me' (featuring a Moby impersonator) and a solo 'Stan'.

8 MILES HIGH

In 2002 Eminem would make it on to the silver screen in *8 Mile* as Hollywood attempted to give fans a detailed account of his life to date. The semi-autobiographical movie was directed by Curtis Hanson, famed for his work on *The Hand That Rocked The Cradle* and *LA Confidential* in the 1990s.

Hollywood stars were also brought out in force in the form of Kim Basinger and Brittany Murphy as Marshall's mother and girlfriend respectively. Eminem played Jimmy 'Rabbit' Smith, a white rapper growing up in Detroit who is disillusioned with his life. Growing up in such a tough neighbourhood, rap is his release, but he suffers from stage fright and has to overcome his anxieties to make it. The film netted more than $200 million at the box office and spawned one of Em's biggest hits, 'Lose Yourself', which topped the charts in 14 countries.

'Eminem delights fans with his onstage antics that see him play up his aggressive persona, frequently lampooning various stars who have been unfortunate enough to end up in his songs.' AMAZON.COM REVIEW

'People ask me, "Well, how do we know when you're joking and when you're serious? 'Cos you say you don't mean everything you say, but some things you say you mean." It's like, you don't. That's the mystique about me.'

EMINEM

MOVIE FALLOUT

The film *8 Mile* was well received by fans, but coolly by critics and the movie business. One sample review said, 'The film is really no more than a two-hour prelude to a climax in which our hero ... rhythmically tells people off', though the *Chicago Sun-Times* broke ranks, stating that 'We are hardly started in *8 Mile*, and already we see that this movie stands aside from routine debut films by pop stars ... Like Prince's *Purple Rain*, it is the real thing.'

The following year's Golden Globe Awards gave the film only one nomination – Best Original Song for 'Lose Yourself' – but Eminem had the last laugh when the song won an Academy

'We sat down with Scott Silver going through things that happened in my life and him just writing the script and getting what he took from me. It's symbolic to anyone who's trying to make it in the music business.' EMINEM

'We are **aware** of the **lyric** and are in the **process** of determining what **action,** if any, will be taken. The **Secret Service** takes every potential **threat** against the **President** seriously. We don't have the **luxury** to do **otherwise.**'

SECRET SERVICE SPOKESMAN

Award in that very same category. The *8 Mile* soundtrack on which it appeared was certified quadruple platinum in January 2003. And later that year MTV recognized him with two Movie Awards for Best Actor and Best Breakthrough Performance. Like Madonna, who tried to diversify into movies in earlier years, he had found that, while the fans bought into his big-screen fantasies, he would not receive credit from an industry to which he was, as he so often found himself, an 'outsider'.

UNDER INVESTIGATION

At the tail end of 2003 an unfinished Eminem track leaked online and spread like wildfire via online chat rooms and peer-to-peer downloading websites. Some 18 months had passed since the release of *The Eminem Show* and fans were eager for a taste of some new material. However, the unfinished bootleg caught some unwanted attention, namely from the US Secret Service.

The government organization was interested in one lyric in particular, where Marshall raps: 'F#©k money/I don't rap for dead presidents/I'd rather see the president dead'. Agents wanted to discover whether it threatened the then-president George Bush's life. However, the investigation went nowhere and the finished article, eventually titled 'We As Americans', ended up as a bonus track on Eminem's 2004 album *Encore*.

'This was an unfinished song,' said an Eminem spokesman. 'There was no determination where, when, how or if it was going to be used.'

EM TAK∃S
AN ENCORE

Originally set for release on 16 November 2004 but moved four days earlier – coincidentally, exactly eight years to the day his debut album, *Infinite*, was released – *Encore* made music-business history in becoming the first album to sell 10,000 digital copies in one week. Eminem was, at the time he recorded *Encore*, beginning to form an addiction to prescription drugs, and he has since said that he is not pleased with the album. Certainly the lyrical content was simpler and markedly less controversial than its predecessors, but then maybe that had something to do with the rap wave that had followed in Eminem's wake – he had been a trailblazer, but was it reasonable to expect him to shock as he did in the old days?

On the song 'Talkin' 2 Myself' featured in later album *Recovery* (2010), Eminem stated the album 'doesn't count' due to his drug addiction. *Encore* nevertheless earned Eminem three Grammy Award nominations at the 48th Annual Grammy Awards: tellingly, though, it became the only major Eminem studio album not to win a Best Rap Album award, losing to Kanye West's *Late Registration* (2005).

JOSTLING WITH JACKO

'Just Lose It' was the lead single from Eminem's 2004 studio album *Encore*, and the track would become infamous for its video. At a time when pop superstar Michael Jackson was facing a long court case, Eminem –

'People can **decipher** it how they **wanna**. But it's not actually **Michael Jackson,** it's **me** playing Michael Jackson, studying the **moves** and **doing** the **impressions.** I don't have an **opinion,** really...'

EMINEM

ever the showman – chose the video to mock the man dubbed 'The King of Pop', aiming to usher in a new generation of music artists.

The video sees Eminem parody Jacko's 'Billie Jean' video, and an incident from the 1980s when his hair caught fire while filming a Pepsi commercial. Unsurprisingly, the video created a wave of criticism, with some TV stations banning its screening. Ever defiant, Eminem dismissed the criticism and the video went viral on the internet. 'Just Lose It' has since clocked up more than 32 million views on Eminem's YouTube channel.

BADMOUTHING BUSH

If 'Just Lose It' brought out the playful child in Eminem, 'Mosh' showed him in full political mode, displaying his displeasure at the regime running the US. While President George Bush was no stranger to criticism during his eight-year tenure, 'Mosh' and its accompanying video are particularly pointed.

'I knew we had the potential to say something that would be heard by the masses. Mr Mathers had also been in the lab concocting his own plans for the election and it was precisely the anthem I had been looking for.'

GUERRILLA NEWS NETWORK

The track was released just before the 2004 presidential election and the animated video was created by activist media firm Guerrilla News Network, and released online. Depicting Eminem's dissatisfaction with the Bush regime and the war in Iraq, it was described by *The Nation*'s Sam Graham-Felsen as possibly 'one of the most overtly political videos ever produced'. Eminem was urging his fans to vote President Bush out of office. Although Eminem was ultimately unsuccessful in that aim, the world saw a more engaged side to Marshall Mathers.

TAKIN' A BREAK

After a turbulent relationship with the mother of his two daughters, Kimberley Scott, the pair embarked on the next chapter of their relationship in 2006 as they remarried. However, this period was marred by ongoing personal problems in Eminem's life that ultimately led him to take a career break. He released the aptly named *Curtain Call* in 2005, featuring some of his greatest hits.

Internet forums were abuzz with rumours about Eminem's next move, many believing he would remain behind the scenes in the studio as a producer rather than an artist. The album was originally thought to be titled *The Funeral*, only adding fuel to the flames of speculation. The online buzz must have helped, as the compilation CD soared straight to No.1 in the US and UK, despite featuring just four new songs.

'I'm at a point in my life right now where I feel like I don't know where my career is going. This is the reason that we called [the new CD] Curtain Call, because this could be the final thing. We don't know.' EMINEM

'I used to get pills wherever I could. I was just taking anything that anybody was giving to me. Even when they told me I almost died, it didn't click.' EMINEM

TOUR CANCƎLLATIONS

The year of 2005 was notable in Eminem's history for all the wrong reasons. The *Detroit Free Press* reported that Eminem would be retiring from touring and recording, stating that his last concert would take place in Dublin on 17 September. Eminem later told MTV that he wasn't retiring, but was going to take a break from his own music to produce other artists. The truth of the matter was somewhat different – he cancelled his European tour scheduled for that summer citing exhaustion, and was then hospitalized for a reported dependency on sleep medication. Things were clearly not right, and millions of fans worldwide had their fingers crossed. It took two stays in rehab for him to finally kick the habit. The experience gave him an insight into his mother's problems. He said, 'Now that I understand that I'm an addict, I definitely have compassion for my mother. I get it.'

...AND HOSPITALIZATIONS

The first period of rehab took place in Brighton, Michigan, but the experience was so uncomfortable that he chose to spend his second spell detoxing in a normal hospital. The reason he couldn't go back to rehab was that he 'felt like Bugs Bunny'. He says, '... when Bugs Bunny walks into rehab, people are going to turn and look. People were stealing my hats and pens and notebooks and asking for autographs. I couldn't concentrate on my problem.'

As he later told British TV chat-show host Jonathan Ross: 'I just wasn't taking care of myself. I was in a dark place. I got sober but it was pretty rough. A couple of years were bad for me.' He admitted that, at the time, he even considered suicide – 'at times I wanted to just give it up' – but pulled through by strength of character.

'Rap was my drug. It used to get me high and then it stopped getting me high. Then I had to resort to other things to make me feel that … now rap's getting me high again.' EMINEM

FIGHTING HIS DEMONS

Eminem allowed very few outside his inner circle of trusted friends to share the mental and physical problems he was fighting. Consequently, news of his life was rare and eagerly seized on when he did break cover. In September 2007, he

called New York radio station Hot 97 during an interview with 50 Cent and said he was 'in limbo' and 'debating' about when and if he would release another album. He said, 'I'm always working – I'm always in the studio. It feels good right now, the energy of the label. For a while, I didn't want to go back to the studio … I went through some personal things. I'm coming out of those [and] it feels good.'

In September 2008, Eminem made an appearance on his Sirius satellite radio channel, Shade 45, in which he confirmed music was playing a part in the healing process. 'You know, the more I keep producing, the better it seems like I get 'cause I just start knowing stuff.'

MARSHALL RETURNS

Having been rarely seen since the release of *Curtain Call*, Eminem set fans' tongues wagging in December 2008 when he revealed that he was to make a new record of original material – and, what's more, Dr. Dre would once again be at the helm. However, the landscape of music was shifting from physical product to distribution via the internet (as he found out the hard way after a demo of a track was leaked online).

The unrefined track, which would later become 'Crack A Bottle', was at such an early stage, including unused lyrics and even featured Marshall rapping Dr. Dre's cameo. The leaking appeared to work in Eminem's favour, with the net abuzz with talk of his impending return – this he accomplished with *Relapse* (2009).

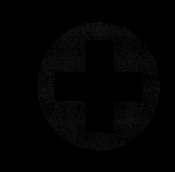

'It wasn't close to finished [...]. It's like someone catches you[,] peeping in your window before you got the Spiderman costume all zipped up! Nobody is supposed to see that.' EMINEM

'There's some **celebrity bashing** in it - I wanna say it's **not** necessarily intentional **bashing,** it's not necessarily taking **deliberate shots** at people...Yes it is, what am I talking about?!' EMINEM

POKING MORE FUN

Eminem announced his return to the frontline of hip-hop with *Relapse*, and the album's lead single was exactly what fans had hoped for and to an extent even expected – Marshall handing it to a slew of celebrities and giving his own unique take on pop culture. No one was safe in 'We Made You' as Eminem targeted everyone from Jessica Simpson to US politician Sarah Palin.

Though some would argue that the dozen celebs that fell victim to Marshall's acid tongue was the highlight of his return, it was the accompanying video that really rammed it home. Directed by Joseph Kahn, who had headed the notorious 'Without Me' video, the video for 'We Made You' saw Em cavort with a fuller-figured Jessica Simpson impersonator and have a dinner date with a lookalike of TV star Kim Kardashian, while Marshall and Dre even appear on Star Trek's starship *Enterprise*. It was unsurprising, then, that the video has amassed nearly 50 million views on Eminem's official YouTube channel.

HE'S NO TWIT

Eminem was taught some harsh lessons in the nature of online music early on with the leaking of various tracks on chatrooms and peer-to-peer sites, but he decided to turn the relationship between artist and internet on its head in 2009 when he used micro-blogging website Twitter to stir up interest in his forthcoming album, *Relapse*.

After using the website to reveal the album's cover, Marshall also teased his followers in the weeks leading up to the album's May release with a series of cryptic Tweets depicting a nightmarish fictional world in which he is unable to recover from his addictions. His fans were on tenterhooks, eager for morsels of information on their idol's next move. He also used Twitter to give fans clues about where to find exclusive tickets to the album's launch in various locations around his home town of Detroit. After falling victim to net-savvy pirates in the past, nearly a decade later it was now Eminem who held all the online cards.

UNLIKELY FRIENDSHIPS

As he geared up for his return to the spotlight, Eminem revealed the identity of a man who helped him get back on his feet, and no, it wasn't one of his D-12 crew, 50 Cent or even Dr. Dre. The man was flamboyant superstar Elton John. The pair had performed a special version of 'Stan' at the 2001 Grammy Awards, and that was where the unlikely duo hit it off. 'We became friends and I talk to him about things, career-wise.'

The Grammy performance came amid criticism of Marshall for what some perceived as homophobic lyrics, but the performance, which ended in a hug and a show of mutual appreciation, turned those opinions on their heads. 'I think it made a statement in itself saying that he understood where I was coming from.' Eminem later said, 'If you really think that about me, you really don't know Marshall.'

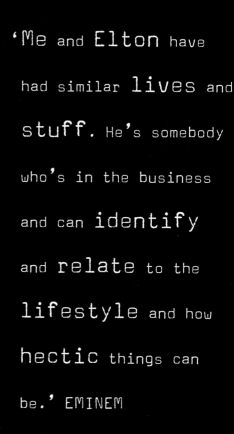

'Me and Elton have had similar lives and stuff. He's somebody who's in the business and can identify and relate to the lifestyle and how hectic things can be.' EMINEM

'Nothing that I do or say or wish is gonna bring Proof back. I don't know if I can ever totally accept his death. But I'm certainly getting better at coping with it.' EMINEM

DJ PROOF: RIP

One of the many personal things Marshall Mathers had to deal with in the Noughties was the violent death in 2006 of D-12 member and long-time childhood friend DJ Proof. The pair had known each other since they were 12 years old and lived on the same block, although they attended different schools. He appeared in the film *8 Mile* (although in the film the character based on him, Future, was portrayed by Mekhi Phifer) and played Lil' Tic, a freestyle rapper who rap-battles with the character played by Eminem.

Real name DeShaun Holton, Proof was killed in a Detroit club fight that broke out over a game of pool and escalated to firearms. Proof's death was mentioned on *Relapse* in the songs 'Deja Vu' and 'Beautiful', and on the 2010 album *Recovery* in 'Going Through Changes' and 'You're Never Over'. A tribute to Proof by Eminem, titled 'Difficult' and later to be called 'Doody', was leaked online at the end of 2010.

TWEET NOTHINGS

If the leaking of 'Crack A Bottle' was a crash course in the online music landscape for Eminem, then the announcement of his seventh studio album showed that the tables had turned. Marshall had promised a sequel to his successful comeback album, *Relapse*, as he had too much material for just one CD. However, he whipped his five million Twitter followers into a frenzy in less than 140 characters when he tweeted in April 2010: 'There is no *Relapse 2*.'

With thousands of fans retweeting his statement, Eminem had the attention of the masses as he followed his tweet with one word: 'RECOVERY'. The announcement and album name change signified a turnaround in Marshall's life, and he wanted the message to go direct to his fans.

OVERCOMING THE BLOCK

Eminem had, he later revealed, gone through a two-year period where he had writer's block and could barely write anything. And anything he recorded didn't meet the high standards he had set himself. 'It was never good enough. I would sit down and listen to it over and over again, trying to find something good about it. And it just felt to me like … well, I always had the reaction of 'Uhhh, this is *not* me!''

Having overcome that problem, he now wanted to deliver more material to the fans, teaming up not only with Dr. Dre but other producers, including Just Blaze, to go in 'a completely

'As I kept recording and working with new producers, a sequel to Relapse started to make less and less sense, and I wanted to make a completely new album. I think it deserves its own title.' EMINEM

different direction which made me start from scratch'.
He says, 'The new tracks started to sound very different
than the tracks I originally intended to be on *Relapse 2* …'

SOCIAL CRUTCHES

When Eminem disappeared in 2006, struggling to deal with
the death of his good friend and fellow rapper Proof, it was the
culmination of a tough childhood and perhaps also a tough life
in the public eye. Fans wanted a piece of him, the media
thought they knew him, and controversy and criticism were
lurking behind every corner.

Fast-forward to the late Noughties and stars' relationships
with both fans and media alike is vastly different. Social
networks such as Twitter and Facebook enable fans to
feel closer to their idols, while also giving celebrities a
direct voice, to make or break news, or even generate
excitement. Never one to fall behind, Eminem has taken
to both Facebook and Twitter, becoming one of the most
influential celebs on the web.

TELLING HIS OWN STORY

Eminem published his autobiography, titled *The Way I Am* in
October 2008 and tells of his early struggles with poverty all
the way through to drugs, fame and his recent depression. As
well as commenting on past controversies, *The Way I Am* also
showcases Eminem's songs, with in-depth discussions of his
writing process and his work in the studio with Dr. Dre.

'I was doing little exercises to come out of that writer's block, like writing a new rhyme a day and trying to do little exercises, like mental things to just get me out of it.' EMINEM

Original lyrics for hits such as 'Lose Yourself' and 'Stan' appeared alongside personal snapshots, illustrations by Eminem himself and concert flyers.

Add to this a visual tour of his Detroit haunts and behind-the-scenes photos from tours and it was clear this was more than just another book on Eminem – it was the whole amazing story in his own words, as if he were talking to the reader across the table. This was a must-buy, even for fans who had not read a book since their schooldays, and appeared in many Christmas stockings come the end of 2008.

'This is the ultimate scrapbook for fans. It's not just Eminem giving people an insight and his own thoughts on his journey so far, but lots of cool archive material.'

ZANE LOWE, RADIO 1

'I don't think the subjects on this record call for, you know, chainsaws and axes out and murder everyone. I think consciously I went in a different direction.'

EMINEM

RECOVERY COMPLETE

The emotional turmoil Eminem had to overcome in the mid-Noughties seemed to have renewed his inspiration. 'My music was always the outlet for me to get through whatever I was going through at the time,' he said in 2009, adding, 'when I put it down on paper, and when I say it in the studio, it's always been therapy for me.' *Relapse* brought him back to Grammy-winning form, while *Recovery* (2010) would be the world's bestselling album of the year with over 3.4 million copies sold in the US alone.

The *Recovery* album featured two covers: one showed Eminem walking down a country road and the other sitting in a transparent living room in the middle of Detroit with the Renaissance Center in the background. The inner sleeve showed pictures of Eminem praying and without a shirt. The album is dedicated '2 anyone who's in a dark place tryin' 2 get out. Keep your head up ... It does get better!'

RULING FACEBOOK

Eminem's return to the spotlight in 2009 following his personal problems could be considered one of the most successful comebacks of recent times. With both *Relapse* and *Recovery* topping the US and UK charts, the appetite for Marshall and his music appeared unabated.

One of the most notable aspects of his return was his heightened presence online. To date he has clocked up nearly

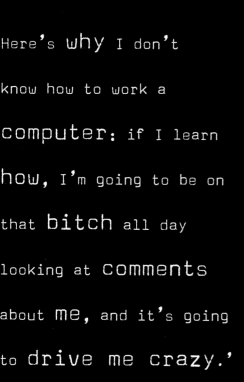

Here's **why** I don't know how to work a **computer**: if I learn **how,** I'm going to be on that **bitch** all day looking at **comments** about **me,** and it's going to **drive me crazy.'**

EMINEM

six million followers on Twitter, and in 2011 he surpassed pop superstar Lady Gaga to become the most 'liked' living celebrity on Facebook, with nearly 29 million fans opting to show their appreciation for the rapper on the popular social network.

To date, Eminem has soared to more than 46 million 'likes', making him the top liked celebrity, living or dead. And by amassing approximately 50,000 more likes daily, that doesn't look set to change any time soon. However, despite his online influence, down-to-earth Marshall concedes he doesn't even know how to operate a computer.

NOT AFRAID

'Not Afraid' was Eminem's comeback single, released in April 2010, and was a song with a message. *Rolling Stone* magazine remarked, 'Over a dark, operatic beat, Eminem delivers rhymes that are typically acrobatic – and typically heavy-handed. But the anger has a gathering quality.'

The single became the 16th song in the history of the Billboard Hot 100 to debut at No. 1, but only the second hip-hop single to achieve the feat following 'I'll Be Missing You' by Puff Daddy and Faith Evans featuring 112.

'Not Afraid' sold 380,000 digital downloads in its first week, while the music video, directed by Rich Lee and shot in Newark, New Jersey, won the MTV Video Music Award for Best Male Video at the 2010 MTV Video Music Awards.

ROCKING WITH RIHANNA

The surest sign of a revitalized Eminem was his renewed willingness to collaborate with others. The musical marriage between Eminem and Rihanna in 2010 worked to perfection, giving Eminem his biggest-selling single since 'The Real Slim Shady' and allowing Rihanna to put the temporary sales blip that was her *Rated R* album (2009) behind her.

The song 'Love The Way You Lie' was the second single to be taken from *Recovery*. It was a US chart-topper and reached No. 2 in the UK after its August 2010 release, spending some 43 weeks on the chart as proof of its longevity. It earned nominations for Grammy Awards, Billboard Music Awards, MuchMusic Video Awards and others.

Critics speculated that the video may have been related to the personal relationships of Eminem and Rihanna with Kimberley Scott (Kim Mathers) and Chris Brown respectively; director Joseph Khan dismissed that, however.

'I want people just to be able to identify with the characters and recognize that two people are together that are completely wrong for each other and things spiral out of control ...'

JOSEPH KHAN

'Eminem's devastating set confirmed his status as the modern-day Elvis. Eminem is so lean and rangy now that, as he rampages through 30 songs, it's hard to see where all these words can be coming from.'

DAILY TELEGRAPH

V FOR VICTORY

Eminem's performances at the V Festival's Weston Park and Chelmsford sites in August 2011 earned him not only a rapturous reaction from fans, but also a cool £2 million fee. He chose to play the British festival as an alternative to lucrative gigs at other venues. A source told *The Sun* newspaper, 'Eminem is a smart guy. H[e] and his management know they'll make cash quicker and without the hassle of organizing and promoting gigs. He has few overheads. He only needs roadies and a DJ.'

As well as wowing the crowds with his own hits, Eminem was joined on stage first by collaborators D-12 for 'Fight Music' and, later, Rihanna to perform their hit 'Love The Way You Lie', after the Barbadian singer had appeared earlier in the day. This inspired a sea of lighter flames before Em closed the show and the festival with hits 'My Name Is', 'Stan' and, finally, the anthemic 'Not Afraid'.

AWARDS APLENTY

Eminem's return to the rap scene saw him pick up every award for which he was eligible. He won Grammy Awards in 2011 for Best Rap Album (*Recovery*) and Best Rap Solo Performance ('Not Afraid'), and was nominated for Album of the Year (*Recovery*), Record of the Year, Song of the Year, Best Rap/Sung Collaboration, Best Rap Song (awarded to the songwriter), and Best Music Video, Short Form

'I'm back at a point where I'm having fun again with rap. For a few years there, I lost my way … I forgot how to have fun with it. And I'm just now learning how to do that again.'

EMINEM

('Love The Way You Lie' with Rihanna), Best Pop Collaboration with Vocals ('Airplanes Part II' with B.o.B and Hayley Williams), and Best Rap Song ('Not Afraid').

Going further back into his history, *The Marshall Mathers LP* and *The Eminem Show* were this year certified 10 times platinum, while the video for latest release 'Love The Way You Lie' was nominated for four MTV Video Music Awards – Best Male Video, Best Direction, Best Cinematography, and Best Video with a Message.

THE FUTURE

After a period of extreme turbulence, the life of Marshall Mathers, alias Eminem, appears to be stable and on track once more. Perhaps, on turning 40 in 2012, Eminem could be excused a smile of self-satisfaction. He is now something of a family man, having adopted two other daughters: Alaina 'Lainie' Mathers, the child of Kimberley Scott's sister, and Whitney, Scott's child from a previous relationship. He is also the legal guardian of his half-brother, Nathan.

Now proudly sober, he says 'hanging out with my kids and watching TV' is his biggest vice. 'Not really anything spectacular. I get up in the mornings and I run. I run quite a bit these days.' He is fit, healthy and ready to prove that a white kid from Detroit still has something relevant to say, even in middle age.

'Anything I've ever said I certainly was feeling at the time. But I think I've calmed down a bit. My overall look on things is a lot more mature than it used to be.' EMINEM

FURTHER INFORMATION

EMINEM VITAL INFO

Birth Name   Marshall Bruce Mathers III

Birth Date   17 October 1972

Birth Place   St Joseph, Missouri, USA

Height   1.7 m (5 ft 8 in)

Nationality   American

Hair Colour   Previously bleached blond, now brown

Eye Colour   Blue

Alter-Egos   Eminem, Slim Shady, Ken Kaniff
(previous creation of rapper Aristotle)

DISCOGRAPHY

Infinite (1996)

The Slim Shady LP (1999)

The Marshall Mathers LP (2000)

The Eminem Show (2002)

Encore (2004)

Relapse (2009)

Recovery (2010)

NO. 1 SINGLES*

2000:   'The Real Slim Shady'
             'Stan'

2002:   'Without Me'
             'Lose Yourself'

2004:   'Just Lose It'

2005:   'Like Toy Soldiers'
             'When I'm Gone'

2006:   'Smack That'

2009:   'Crack A Bottle'
             'We Made You'

2010:   'Not Afraid'
             'Love The Way You Lie'

* Worldwide

AWARDS

ACADEMY AWARD

2003: Best Original Song 'Lose Yourself'

BRIT AWARDS

2001: Best International Male Solo Artist

2003: Best International Male Solo Artist

Best International Album *The Eminem Show*

2005: Best International Male Solo Artist

GRAMMY AWARDS

2000: Best Rap Album *The Slim Shady LP*

Best Solo Rap Performance 'My Name Is'

2001: Best Rap Album *The Marshall Mathers LP*

Best Solo Rap Performance 'The Real Slim Shady'

Best Rap Performance by a Duo or Group

'Forgot About Dre'

2003: Best Rap Album *The Eminem Show*

Best Short Form Music Video 'Without Me'

2004: Best Male Rap Solo Performance 'Lose Yourself'

Best Rap Song 'Lose Yourself'

2010: Best Rap Album *Relapse*

Best Rap Performance by a Duo or Group

'Crack A Bottle'

2011: Best Rap Album *Recovery*

Best Male Rap Solo Performance 'Not Afraid'

MTV VIDEO MUSIC AWARDS

1999: Best New Artist 'My Name Is'

2000: Best Rap Video 'Forgot About Dre'

Video of the Year 'The Real Slim Shady'

Best Male Video 'The Real Slim Shady'

2002: Video of the Year 'Without Me'

Best Male Video 'Without Me'

Best Rap Video 'Without Me'

Best Direction 'Without Me'

2003: Best Video from A Film 'Lose Yourself'

2009: Best Hip-Hop Video 'We Made You'

2010: Best Male Video 'Not Afraid'

Best Hip-Hop Video 'Not Afraid'

MUSIC OF BLACK ORIGIN AWARDS (MOBOS)

2010: Best International Act

ONLINE

eminem.com: Official site with news, tour dates, biographical information, forums, photos and more

eminemworld.com: unofficial site with pictures, lyrics and message boards

trshady.com: fansite with lyrics, downloads, news, a forum and more

eminem.net: everything you ever wanted to know about Eminem by fans for fans

facebook.com/eminem: sign up to read Eminem's latest Wall postings

@Eminem: follow all Marshall Mathers' antics on Twitter

BIOGRAPHIES

MICHAEL HEATLEY [AUTHOR]

Michael Heatley edited the acclaimed *History of Rock* partwork.
He is the author of over 100 music biographies, as well as books on
sport and TV. His acclaimed biography of late DJ John Peel sold over
100,000 copies, while *Michael Jackson – Life Of A Legend 1958–2009*
topped the Sunday Times bestseller lists and has been widely translated.

PRIYA ELAN [FOREWORD]

Priya Elan is a leading music and entertainment journalist. He has
written for a number of publications including *The Guardian*, *The Times*,
The Financial Times, *Mojo* and *Grazia*. He is currently the Assistant
Editor of NME.com.

PICTURE CREDITS